After School

Nonstandard Measurement

Aubrie Nielsen

Consultants

Chandra C. Prough, M.S.Ed.
National Board Certified
Newport-Mesa
  Unified School District

Jodene Smith, M.A.
ABC Unified School District

Publishing Credits

Dona Herweck Rice, *Editor-in-Chief*
Lee Aucoin, *Creative Director*
Chris McIntyre, M.A.Ed., *Editorial Director*
James Anderson, M.S.Ed., *Editor*
Aubrie Nielsen, M.S.Ed., *Associate Education Editor*
Neri Garcia, *Senior Designer*
Stephanie Reid, *Photo Editor*
Rachelle Cracchiolo, M.S.Ed., *Publisher*

Image Credits

p.4 Rich Legg/iStockphoto; p.8 Getty Images/Comstock Images; p.12 kali9/iStockphoto; p.16 Michael DeLeon/iStockphoto; p.20 Kim Gunkel/iStockphoto; p.23 (top) Judy Barranco/iStockphoto; p. 26 Gerville Hall/iStockphoto; pp.26-27 Christian Uhrig/iStockphoto; p.28 photos1st/iStockphoto; All other images: Shutterstock.

Teacher Created Materials

5301 Oceanus Drive
Huntington Beach, CA 92649-1030
http://www.tcmpub.com
ISBN 978-1-4333-3440-5
© 2012 Teacher Created Materials, Inc.

Table of Contents

What do you do after school?

Try to **measure**! It is fun to do.

He likes to play the violin.

How **long** is the violin?

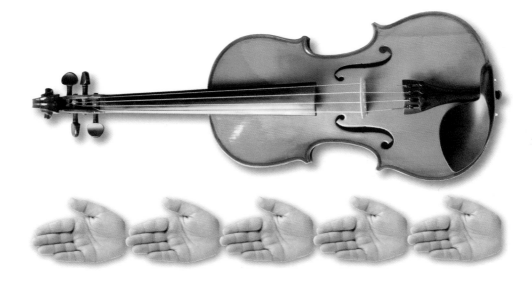

It is 5 hands long.

They take
dance class.

How long is the shoe?

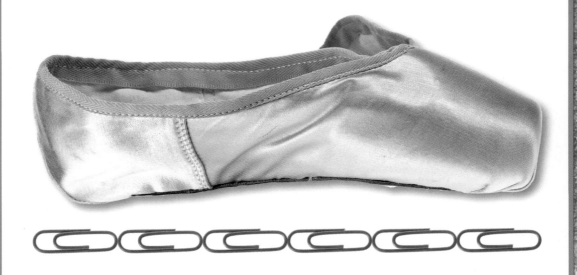

It is 6 paper clips long.

She likes to swim.

How **wide** is one lane?

It is 7 flippers wide.

They play soccer.

How wide is the field?

It is 8 coaches wide.

She plays the piano.

How **tall** is the piano?

It is 6 shoes tall.

They play basketball.

How tall is the hoop?

It is 10 balls tall.

He does his homework.

How **heavy** is his backpack?

It **weighs** as much as 3 books.

She likes to paint.

How heavy is the paint?

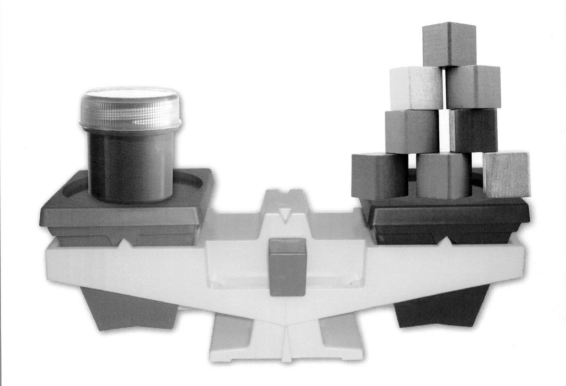

It weighs as much as 8 blocks.

What things can you measure after school?

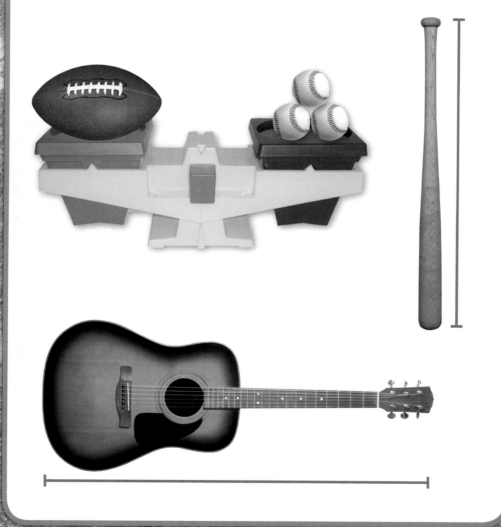

He rides his bike.

How tall is the bike? Measure in helmets.

She takes karate class.

How wide is her belt? Use tools to measure.

What can you measure in your classroom?

Materials
- ✓ paper
- ✓ pencil
- ✓ object to measure
- ✓ tools for measuring

1 Find an object in your classroom.

2 Find tools to use to measure.

3 Measure your object.
- How long is it?
- How wide is it?
- How tall is it?
- How heavy is it?

Glossary

heavy—a measurement of how much an object weighs

long—a measurement from end to end

measure—to find out how long, tall, wide, or heavy an object is

tall—a measurement from top to bottom

weighs—measures how heavy an object is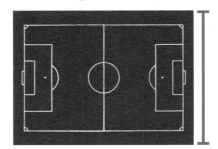

wide—a measurement of the shorter side of an object

You Try It!

Pages 24–25:
Five (5) helmets tall

Pages 26–27:
Answers will vary. Possibilities include one (1) paper clip or three (3) centimeter cubes, but students can use any object to measure.

Solve the Problem

Answers will vary based on the objects used.